$1.00

D0981218

OVER COMING

LIFE'S CHALLENGES

LESSONS FROM THE LIFE OF JOSEPH

BILL CROWDER

Discovery House.
from Our Daily Bread Ministries

Requests for permission to quote from this book should
be directed to: Permissions Department, Discovery House
P.O. Box 3566, Grand Rapids, MI 49501.

Scripture quotations are from The New King James
Version, © 1982 by Thomas Nelson, Inc.
All rights reserved.

Cover photophy: Getty Images/Alexander W Helin
Getty Images/Bulgac

Printed in the United States of America
07 08 09 10 / 10 9 8 7 6 5 4 3 2 1

Contents

Introduction

The football coach had reached the point of exasperation: "Losing five games in a row is bad enough. But what really frustrates me is that we keep making the same mistakes over and over. We just aren't learning anything!"

Wasting the pain of failure or defeat happens off the playing field as well. We can be slow to learn that what causes the most pain is not the initial loss or hardship but the failure to learn anything in the process. A friend shared with me the frustration of a colleague of his who had been passed over for a promotion. In fact, the colleague was so upset by the snub that he went to the administrator responsible for the decision and demanded explanation. "How can you ignore my qualifications?" he said. "I have twenty-five years of experience!" The administrator's response was both candid and penetrating. "No, you don't have twenty-five years of experience. You have had one year of experience twenty-five times." The man just hadn't learned along the way.

If we really believe, as Romans 8:28 promises, that God is working in and through all things "for good to those who love God," then one of our greatest challenges is to allow hard, painful, and tear-filled experiences to be our teacher in the classroom of life.

One person who learned how to overcome in the midst of extremely difficult circumstances was Joseph, the Old Testament patriarch who went from slavery to international prominence in the ancient world. It is my prayer that by examining the life of this man we can learn some important and valuable lessons for our own lives.

—BILL CROWDER

The Lessons of Life

On one of the old *Happy Days* television programs, teenager Richie Cunningham had just been "grounded for life" by his father for misbehavior. As father and son talked about Richie's misdeed and the punishment, Howard Cunningham asked his son, "Do you know that there is a lesson in this for you?" Richie's response was priceless: "I figured anything with this much pain had to have a lesson in it somewhere."

That is the way real life works! We do not learn the great lessons of life in times of ease and prosperity, comfort and joy. The greatest character-building and faith-strengthening lessons come during times of difficulty and heartache.

When my father died, I had been a pastor for

only a few months, and my father's funeral was the first funeral I preached. At the funeral home, a pastor friend put his arm around my shoulder and said, "I know this hurts an awful lot—and it should. But one day you will be thankful for the lessons you learn this week.

"I have never lost anyone close to me," he continued, "but I have preached scores of funerals. Never in those funerals have I felt that I had the ability to truly comfort people in the time of their greatest loss because I have never experienced that pain myself. What you will learn in your pain, Bill, will enable you to minister far more effectively to the pain of others."

In one of the most practical books in the New Testament, James wrote these words:

> My brethren, count it all joy when you fall into various trials, knowing that the testing of your faith produces patience. But let

patience have its perfect work, that you may be perfect and complete, lacking nothing (1:2–4).

His point is simple: God doesn't waste anything—not even our heartaches and trials. As hard as they may be when we are living through them, they have a purpose in God's eternal plan, and often a major part of that purpose is to help us grow in our faith.

Life has to be lived in forward motion but can only be understood by looking back. This demands that we trust in the loving purposes of a sovereign God. We must trust that He is in control—especially when life seems to be out of control.

> *"Life is an operation which is done in a forward direction. One lives toward the future."*
> —JOSE ORTEGA Y GASSET

11

Paul called this kind of trust "walking by faith" (2 Corinthians 5:7), which goes against every element of self-preservation that is ingrained in us. We want to take charge, manipulate, and control. But God wants us to trust in the love of a Father who makes no mistakes. He wants us to rely on the One who makes us "more than conquerors through Him who loved us" (Romans 8:37).

One shining example of walking by faith in the midst of overwhelming circumstances is the Old Testament character Joseph. From an early age, his life was filled with dark, difficult experiences—tangled threads of hate and betrayal, fear and isolation. Yet Joseph was able, through his unwavering faith in a sovereign God, to rise above all of this and become

> *"Hindsight is always twenty-twenty."*
> —BILLY WILDER

12

a godly man in an ungodly culture—a true overcomer.

His life can teach us much about how to deal with the tangled threads of our own lives.

Overcoming Treachery

There are many beautiful words in the English language—words that are almost musical. *Treachery* is not one of those words.

When we hear the word *treachery*, we think of Benedict Arnold, who sold out his fledgling nation almost before it was born. We hear Caesar, in anguish from the knife planted firmly in his back, cry, "Et tu, Brute?" When we hear the word *treachery*, our thoughts flash back to a garden on a dark night, the voice of a friend, and a kiss of betrayal that sold out the Son of God for thirty pieces of silver.

As we first enter the life of Joseph, he is only seventeen years old and standing at the very threshold of treachery—treachery and betrayal that will rise up out of his own family.

The Seedbed for Tension

I remember years ago making a call on a family that had visited our church. As soon as I entered the house, I sensed the tension in the air. Whether anyone in that family had love for anyone else, I don't know. But it was abundantly clear to me that they did not like one another. In the course of my forty-five minute visit, two things became obvious—the husband and wife were not on speaking terms with each other, and their personal civil war had seeped from their relationship to their children. The room was filled with tension and unspoken resentment—but the facial expressions and tone of voice spoke more than words could have ever expressed. This was a household torn by unhappiness, and, in all likelihood, was not what either the husband or

15

wife had dreamed of years before when they had gotten married.

We assume that families should be places of warmth, love, acceptance, and security. But far too often, instead, they become breeding grounds for anger, resentment, and bitterness. Such was the case with Jacob's household (see Genesis 37).

Lighting the Fuse of Family Anger

The patriarch Jacob, son of Isaac and grandson of Abraham, was learning the hard way that you really do reap what you sow. He had ignored the biblical pattern for marriage in Genesis 2 by taking multiple wives. And when he had children by these two wives (and their handmaids), he ended up with a "blended" family (actually, "unblended" would be closer to the truth) of twelve sons, all vying for position with their father.

The problem was intensified by Jacob's obvious

preference for his second wife, Rachel, and her two sons, Joseph and Benjamin. Joseph, in particular, was "loved more than all his brothers" (Genesis 37:4). This favoritism by their father created serious friction in the family and resulted in Joseph becoming the object of his brothers' jealousy, resentment, and hatred.

> *"All happy families resemble one another, but each unhappy family is unhappy in its own way."*
> —LEO TOLSTOY, *ANNA KARENINA*

In addition, Jacob's less-than-sterling character was being reproduced in many of his sons. Jacob means "conniver," and he lived up (or down) to his name. Long before, he had manipulated his brother Esau into giving up his birthright—the critical first place in line for the family estate—and then (with his mother's help) manipulated his father into giving him the firstborn's blessing—stealing

17

yet again from his own brother. While Jacob was certainly not the only schemer in the family (his wives, Leah and Rachel, made their own contributions to the problem), Jacob displayed a lifestyle of deceit that would stay with him until he died. Consequently, the family was riddled with poor parenting, deception, manipulation, strife, and self-interest. Genesis 37 describes three points of potential combustion in the household:

- Jacob used Joseph to spy on his older brothers, who hated this "favorite son" (v. 2).
- Jacob made a display of his favoritism in the gift of a special tunic (v. 3).
- Jacob's attitude and actions fed the sibling rivalry, but his sons directed their anger at their brother Joseph, not at their father (v. 4).

The conflict between Jacob's children was rooted in the problems between Jacob and his wives. The same situation is seen hundreds of years later in the household of Elkanah, where polygamy produced inevitable competition and conflict between Hannah and Peninnah (see 1 Samuel 1).

Of course polygamy wasn't the only cause of conflict. Any breakdown in the husband-wife relationship has serious spillover effects on all the relationships in the home. And when that troubled relationship is coupled with misguided parenting, the results can be catastrophic.

By showing preference to Joseph, Jacob made two serious errors. First, by elevating him above his brothers as the object of his love and praise, Jacob sent wrong signals to Joseph about his importance and position in the family. Second, by inference Jacob inflicted the pain of rejection on the sons who had once been the object of his attention but were now ignored. In fact, Jacob treated these men more like servants than like sons. The result was a relational powder keg whose fuse was about to be lit.

When families become breeding grounds for hatred, the effects can be destructive and devastating indeed, as seen in this excerpt from a will of a Mr. Donohoe, dated July 1, 1935:

> Unto my two daughters, Frances Marie and Denise Victoria, by reason of their unloving attitudes toward a doting father . . . I leave the sum of $1 each and a father's curse. May their respective lives be filled with misery, unhappiness, and sorrow. May their deaths be soon and of a lingering, torturous nature. May their souls rest in hell and suffer the torments of the damned for eternity.

It's difficult for me to imagine a father writing such words, let alone harboring such hatred toward his own children. But Jacob's lack of wisdom and obedience had resulted in a family filled with similar emotions. He had doused his household with gasoline, and Joseph was about to strike a match!

The Brashness of Youth

As the spoiled favorite, Joseph lived life on a different level than the rest of the family. His experience of special treatment may even have become his expectation for the norm of what life should be. His life of relative ease would have created great resentment in the minds of his brothers—a resentment that would only get worse when Joseph began to have dreams of his own advancement and rise to even greater status.

Joseph's dreams predicted his future rise to greatness. But instead of keeping them to himself and seeking to understand what they might mean for his own life, he flaunted them before his brothers, who already resented and hated him.

In doing this, young Joseph made three critical errors in judgment:

- He lacked *discernment.* He didn't recognize the troubled situation in his family.
- He lacked *sensitivity.* He didn't consider the impact his words and actions would have on family members or the hurt they might cause.
- He lacked *maturity.* While it was true that one day he would have authority over his brothers, his actions proved that he wasn't ready for that yet.

The Fruit of Bitterness (Genesis 37:12–27)

Earlier, Joseph had brought his father a bad report about his brothers. Now, Jacob sent him once again to check on their work and once again to report what he saw. This was like pouring salt into their already wounded egos. The spoiled one,

the special one, the loved one, Joseph was now
their father's appointed overseer of their work!
As such, they resented his very presence. As they
watched "Daddy's favorite" approach, the pressure
of resentment grew into sarcasm and anger, which
quickly turned into a desire to murder him (vv. 18–
19; see also Matthew 5:21–22). Reuben attempted
to intervene on Joseph's behalf but was rebuffed
(vv. 21–22). Finally, they attacked their own brother:

- They took his coat, the symbol of their
  resentment (v. 23).
- They cast him into a pit to remove him
  from their sight (v. 24).
- With hardened hearts, they sat down to
  enjoy a meal while their young brother
  languished alone in a dark pit (v. 25).
- They sold their own brother into slavery,
  deciding to make a profit on his life
  (vv. 25–28).

Treachery had produced unresolved family tension, which, in turn, had produced bitterness. And bitterness bears a terrible fruit.

*   *   *

For those who are familiar with Joseph's story, it is easy to say, "It's okay. Everything will turn out all right in the end." But those who were living it didn't know that.

Look at the immediate pain that flowed from a family eaten up with hate. Reuben mourned for Joseph (and his own lack of courage). The brothers lied to their father, but never escaped their personal guilt (Genesis 42:22).

For Jacob, the deceiver, now had become the deceived. Years before, he had deceived his own father, Isaac, by shedding the blood of an animal and using its hide to trick him out of the blessing that rightly belonged to Jacob's brother Esau. Now, this deceiver had reaped what he had sown. His own sons also killed a goat and spread the blood on Joseph's special coat, convincing Jacob that the son of his love had been mauled to death by a beast. It is likely that the brothers felt that if Joseph was out of the way, perhaps their father would show love to them. But if that was the case, they were badly mistaken. Jacob refused them all, choosing instead to mourn the loss of the son he loved best. The pain he felt at the loss of Joseph was beyond comfort.

It's interesting to note, however, that although Joseph had been sold into slavery, he is the only one who is not described in the text as being troubled. Even though he was enslaved, he was in the best position of them all. He was right where God wanted him so that he could learn the lessons God wanted to teach him—lessons that would one day make him a great leader and enable him to overcome the treachery and betrayal of his own brothers.

Ever faithful, God would take the evil of men in Joseph's life and use it for Joseph's good and for His glory.

Overcoming Temptation

To say that life is filled with temptations is to have, as sportscaster Howard Cosell used to say, "a marvelous grasp of the obvious." To realize, however, that the greatest temptations often come on the heels of great success is to understand the very essence of what makes life so hard. How we handle success says as much, if not more, about us as how we handle failure.

This might seem far from Joseph's experience, but in fact it was to be his next great hurdle. Imagine being sold into slavery—by your own family no less!—and dragged hundreds of miles away to a foreign land with foreign customs, foreign gods, and a foreign language. Those first days in Egypt as a slave must have been brutally difficult for this seventeen-year-old youth. Rather than becoming bitter, however, Joseph chose instead to "bloom where he had been planted." He learned the language and learned the skills, so that, over the course of the next ten years, he was given more and more responsibility, until he was in charge of all his master's household. It must have taken hard work, great determination, and unyielding trust in his God, but Joseph devoted himself to the task at hand and became as successful as a slave could be.

> *"I can resist everything except temptation."*
> —OSCAR WILDE

As a result, Joseph would be challenged with success and the temptations it brings. And in learning to overcome these temptations, he would demonstrate that the lessons of God were starting to take hold in his young but maturing heart.

The Power of Testimony

Joseph's life was about to take a fascinating turn. He had become the property of Potiphar, an officer of Pharaoh (Genesis 37:36).

Potiphar was "captain of the guard" (Genesis 39:1). There is some disagreement among Bible scholars as to what that role was. Some say he was a warden, others believe he was captain of the palace guard, and still others maintain he was captain of the executioners. What we do know is that Potiphar was powerful and wealthy enough to have many servants and slaves (vv. 11, 14). And he had now added Joseph to his collection.

As we have seen, Joseph distinguished himself in his role in Potiphar's household. But his skill and abilities were not what made the difference in his life. It was God's presence that made the difference. Genesis 39:2 says, "The Lord was with Joseph."

Imagine how painful Joseph's life must have

29

been at that point. At age seventeen, he had been torn from his family and sold into slavery—by his own brothers! How easy it would have been for him to become embittered and hate-filled (like his brothers). But that didn't happen. Although Joseph was far from home and in difficult circumstances, the presence of God was very real in his life.

So real, in fact, that "his master saw that the Lord was with him" (Genesis 39:3). Potiphar could not help but recognize the presence of God in the life of this remarkable slave, and that had a dramatic impact on the Egyptian (39:3–6). Imagine how strong Joseph's testimony must have been for Potiphar, who was a pagan, not only to recognize and admire Joseph's character but to attribute it to God rather than to Joseph himself.

The clear implication of the text is that Joseph was not bitter toward his brothers, nor was he enslaved by his circumstances. He was content in the presence of God (see Hebrews 13:5–6;

Philippians 4:10–13). He didn't mourn his disappointment but became useful where he was. And God used that heart of faithfulness and contentment.

Potiphar recognized God's presence with Joseph, and he made the young slave the overseer of his entire household. Joseph supervised all the other servants, handled public relations, oversaw finances, and was responsible for the provisions for the household (valuable training for a later assignment Joseph would receive). And everything Joseph touched was blessed.

31

Now, perhaps ten years after being sold into slavery, Joseph was on top of the world. And now he was more vulnerable than ever to temptation.

The Power of Temptation

Notice the closing words of Genesis 39:6: "Joseph was handsome in form and appearance." He was good-looking and well-built. And now

Potiphar's wife entered the scene. Her response? She "cast longing eyes on Joseph" (v. 7).

Potiphar's wife would have been right at home in modern American culture, with its casual acceptance and approval of premarital sex and extramarital affairs. She had the same mindset. She was attracted to this young man physically and saw nothing wrong with offering herself to him.

But Joseph refused her advances. He had a powerful set of convictions by which he lived, and he refused to be tempted by lust and desire.

It seems obvious that these convictions were not learned from his father, Jacob, nor from his hate-filled brothers, nor from the palace courts of pagan Egypt. These convictions were learned in the presence of God. He not only battled temptation, but he had a battle plan that he would follow as this woman continued to pursue him.

He had the right concerns (vv. 8–9). He was concerned ethically that his actions not hurt

32

others, in this case Potiphar. His master had entrusted him with much, and Joseph refused to violate that trust for a moment of pleasure. He also looked beyond the immediate to the ultimate, recognizing the consequences that such sin would have on his relationship with God (v. 9). He was concerned spiritually, because he understood that all sin is against God. The offer of sensual pleasure was not worth the price tag attached to it.

33

He had the right strategy (v. 10). He avoided contact with Potiphar's wife. Joseph realized that he had to be aware of the lure of sin and avoid its opportunities. He had to be alert and on guard against temptation.

He had the right escape route (v. 12). When Potiphar's wife finally got Joseph alone and boldly tried to lure him, he ran as far as he could as fast as he could. What Samson, David, and Solomon did not do, Joseph did. He fled, keeping the courage of his convictions and his integrity intact. He exemplified Paul's advice to Timothy: "Flee also youthful lusts" (2 Timothy 2:22). He didn't flirt with sin, argue with it, or reason with it. He fled from it.

The question is, in the face of this persistent temptation and with his limited personal spiritual training, how did Joseph resist?

34

- He recognized that he belonged to God.
- He recognized sin's effect on others.
- He recognized sin as defiance against God.

This young man's godly character was continuing to be shaped. In a perfect world (or on a thirty-minute television sitcom), his steadfast convictions would have resulted in everyone living happily ever after. But real life doesn't operate that way. Life in a fallen world seldom rewards right living.

The Power of Revenge

Joseph had a strategy for maintaining his purity, but Potiphar's wife had a strategy as well. Obviously, she was not accustomed to being refused what she wanted. She began by flattering him—after all, Joseph was in charge of everything else that was Potiphar's. Why not enjoy her as well? When he refused, she tried to wear him down—offering herself to him day after day after day. When that failed, she tried to ambush him and force herself upon him! That level of desperation reveals how determined she was to have him as her own. And if she could not . . . well, you've heard about "the fury of a woman scorned."

Joseph was ruled by principles, but Potiphar's wife was ruled by passion. And when she was rebuffed, her passions exploded in anger and revenge. She lied about Joseph to the men of the household, using his abandoned coat as evidence

35

against him (the second time a coat had been used in a lie about Joseph), and she lied about Joseph to her husband (Genesis 39:13–18).

In ancient Egypt, the penalty for adultery was 1,000 lashes, but the penalty for rape was death. And remember, it's possible that Potiphar was the chief executioner. It's also possible that he knew his wife was lying. At the very least, he knew that such an accusation was out of character for this young man. But desperate to save face, Potiphar had Joseph imprisoned (vv. 19–20).

Joseph ended up in jail for doing the right thing. We protest, "It isn't fair!" And that's true. Often life isn't fair. But our responsibility is to do right and leave the consequences to God.

Joseph had responded properly to his enslavement and to his temptation. How would he respond to this unjust imprisonment?

The Presence of God

Once again Joseph found comfort in the presence of his God: "The Lord was with Joseph and showed him mercy" (Genesis 39:21).

It would have been natural for Joseph to think, "Why be good and do right if I end up here?" But Joseph didn't. Instead, he rested in God's presence, and God blessed him, even in prison (vv. 21–23). Once again, he learned what it meant to overcome in the midst of the pains, problems, dangers, and tests of life.

All these things come into focus when we view them through the lens of God's sovereign purpose. Then we can trust His will and know His mercy.

Joseph's character was under construction as he was shaped by adversity, punished by men, and honored by God. Genesis 39 ends the way it began—with Joseph in bondage. Yet through it all, his solid faith in God's control had helped him overcome.

Overcoming Disappointment

In the television series *The West Wing*, the final season showcased a fictional presidential campaign, with Republican Arnold Vinick contesting Democrat Matt Santos for the White House. In a tightly fought battle, the two politicians went down to the wire and, after hours of counting and recounting the ballots, Santos was declared the winner.

The episode following the election tracked the different paths the two men took next. Santos, the new president-elect, surrounded by staffers and media, making critical decisions about cabinet positions and policy directives, was the eye of the storm of activity that is the preparation for a new executive administration. By contrast, Vinick wrestled with the emptiness of being yesterday's news. Far from being involved in the significant shaping of a government, he was forgotten and ignored— and dangerously close to becoming bitter by the disappointment of falling from national personality to afterthought.

It would certainly be understandable if Joseph, like Arnie Vinick, had lapsed into self-pity at this point. But he didn't. Instead, he rose to a position of leadership in prison, and the jailer entrusted everything under his authority to Joseph's care. Why? Because "the Lord was with Joseph and showed him mercy, and He gave him favor in the sight of the keeper of the prison . . . the Lord was with him; and whatever he did, the Lord made it prosper" (Genesis 39:21, 23).

One of the lessons that is critical to

overcoming is the lesson of patience. Although Joseph was unjustly imprisoned, he went about the business of being useful where he was. He faithfully served and patiently waited because he was learning that he was not there by accident.

Because he trusted God, he also knew that he was not forgotten. God not only remembered, but also had a plan for Joseph that included a tour of duty in the prison of Egypt.

In prison, Joseph had a divine appointment.

Disappointment or Divine Appointment

Two of Pharaoh's officials—his royal butler and his royal baker—had offended the ruler. Pharaoh was so angry that he imprisoned them both. In ancient times, intrigue and political assassinations were common, so it was absolutely critical that the palace staff be totally loyal. Somehow these two men had failed Pharaoh, so they were placed in the prison where Joseph was the head steward (Genesis 40:1–3).

Notice who entrusted them to Joseph's care: the captain of the guard, none other than Potiphar himself (v. 4; see 37:36). Joseph accepted the responsibility and began the task of serving these disgraced members of Pharaoh's court.

This was not some cosmic accident. It was not just "a coincidence." God was in control of Joseph's life—as He is in control of our lives. And because He is in control, nothing happens by accident. Everything has a purpose.

When I was in college, I was faced with a dilemma. I was on the soccer team, but I was also a member of a traveling ministry team. A scheduling conflict arose between the two activities, and I had to

> *"Bless you, prison, for having been in my life."*
> —ALEXANDER SOLZHENITSYN

choose between them. I chose the soccer game
and began making arrangements for someone
to substitute for me on the traveling ministry
team. On the day before these conflicting events,
however, I was injured in a soccer game and
forbidden to play in the next game. Quickly I
reversed course and kept my commitment with
the traveling ministry team. On that trip I met
the young woman who would later become my
wife! After the fact, I learned that she had been
a last-minute substitute on the team. So I met
my life partner on a trip that, humanly speaking,
neither of us was supposed to be on.

One of the great joys—and challenges—of life
is to look expectantly for the hand of God in all
of life's circumstances. Joseph and the two royal
officials converged in prison right on schedule for
the perfect plan of God—though, no doubt, none
of them would have chosen those circumstances
for themselves.

A Divine Investment

With these men in his care, Joseph now had a choice to make. Would he simply go through the motions, doing as little as possible? Fulfilling the minimal requirements of service would not be an altogether surprising attitude in someone who had risen high and fallen far. Or, he could, once again, face undeserved hardship with an attitude of confident trust. He could, as he had done when taken as a boy to the home of Potiphar, choose to be useful where he was. He had a choice. He could be consumed with his own grief, or he could become concerned with the suffering of others.

In spite of (or perhaps because of) his own difficulty and hardship, Joseph had become sensitive to others, a quality that he previously lacked. Instead of ignoring the two men, or turning away, thinking, "No one cares about the mistreatment I have received. Why should I care

43

about anyone else?" Joseph looked at the butler and the baker and recognized their hurt and distress.

Joseph's response to the disappointment of unjust imprisonment was both vertical and horizontal.

- Vertical: He didn't allow his circumstances to disrupt his relationship with God.
- Horizontal: He didn't allow his hurt to prevent him from caring about the hurts of others.

Joseph had the maturity, insight, and grace to set aside his personal adversity and help others who were hurting.

Life is filled with disappointment and loss. That's an inescapable fact. But we can be overcomers by refusing to become self-absorbed and self-centered. Instead of wasting our energy in self-pity, we can invest our time in meeting the needs of others.

After a missionary couple in India saw their six children killed, they devoted themselves to raising three hundred foster children. Following a tragic flood at Toccoa Falls, Georgia, a man whose wife and two children had died in the flood said, "Every time I wanted to cry, someone else needed help and I felt compelled to offer. I was so consumed with helping others that I had no time to worry about myself."

Is that how you respond to adversity and disappointment? Or do you become so consumed with your own pain that you are blind to the pain of others? Sensitivity to the needs of others can be deadened by preoccupation with personal disappointment.

Joseph not only noticed the needs of others; he cared and got involved. His concern for his fellow prisoners grew out of true humility and godly character.

Forgotten Again

Joseph interpreted the dreams of the butler and the baker, making sure they knew that it was God who deserved the credit for his understanding (Genesis 40:8–19). This is a notable contrast to his earlier attitude, when he lorded his dreams over his brothers (Genesis 37). Now his trust was in the Lord, not in himself. Joseph asked only that the butler not forget him: "Remember me when it is well with you, and please show kindness to me; make mention of me to Pharaoh, and get me out of this house" (40:14–15).

Three days later, both dreams were fulfilled, exactly as Joseph had interpreted them (vv. 20–22). The chief butler was restored to his position, and the chief baker was executed. And how was Joseph rewarded? "The chief butler did not remember Joseph, but forgot him" (40:23). Earlier, Joseph's purity was rewarded with imprisonment.

Now, he was abandoned and forgotten—for two full years (41:1).

Once again, it would have been easy for him to succumb to disillusionment and disappointment. But Joseph did not put his trust in men; Joseph's trust was in the Lord. Even though the butler had forgotten Joseph, God hadn't forgotten him—and Joseph knew that and trusted in that.

James 1:2–4 says that the indispensable character quality of patient trust can be learned only through trials. James teaches that without patience there will be no maturity; and without trials, delays, and disappointments there will be no patience.

Joseph had overcome treachery, temptation, and, now, disappointment. The lessons of becoming an overcomer were shaping his life, and he was finally ready for God to use him in a special way.

47

Overcoming the Past

Years ago, Erwin Lutzer wrote a helpful little book titled *Failure: The Back Door to Success.* It could have been written about Joseph. Many times, it takes years of failures and setbacks to become an "overnight success."

Abraham Lincoln is a classic example. He had two failed businesses, one nervous breakdown, endured the death of a sweetheart, and was defeated for public office no fewer than ten times over the space of almost thirty years. Then, incredibly, he was elected President of the United States. His years of failure had equipped him to deal with the heady air of the heights of power and the circumstances he would face during the years of his presidency.

Repeated reversals, apparent failures, and personal tragedies did not defeat Lincoln. Instead, they strengthened his character and commitment. And so it was with Joseph. After thirteen years of reversals, failure, and tragedy, the light of day finally entered his cell.

"Praise God for the hammer, the file, and the furnace. The hammer molds us, the file sharpens us, and the fire tempers us."
—SAMUEL RUTHERFORD

Now, in God's perfect timing, that for which Joseph had been prepared had arrived. The servant and the task converged in a moment in time.

Dreams You Would Like to Forget

At crucial moments in Joseph's life, dreams had played a significant part—first his own dreams and later the dreams of the butler and

49

the baker. Now, once again, God uses dreams to bring Joseph to a turning point. In fact, the three pairs of dreams are all connected in the purposes of God:

- The dreams of the baker and butler (Genesis 40) put Joseph in a position to hear;
- The dreams of Pharaoh (Genesis 41), which made possible the fulfillment of
- The dreams of Joseph (Genesis 37) and his position of authority and rulership.

God was in it all, preparing the way for His purposes in the life of His young servant.

Pharaoh, the ruler of all Egypt, had two dreams that troubled him greatly. Sensing that these were not ordinary dreams, he called for the wisest men of his kingdom to interpret them (Genesis 41:8).

Pharaoh was troubled by spiritual things that were beyond his grasp. But because his wise men and magicians didn't know the God who was dealing with him, their answers were inadequate for the turmoil in his heart.

This points us to a significant principle for spiritual living: There is great danger in seeking spiritual answers in the wrong places. Spiritual hunger and a vacuum of spiritual truth can make people easy prey for the ear-tickling deception of cultists, false teachers, and false spiritual leaders. But the empty answers of false teachers cannot address true spiritual needs or answer the burning spiritual questions of the human heart.

The failure of Pharaoh's wisest men set the stage for God's glory to be revealed through a common slave. What was beyond human reason was not beyond the all-knowing God.

A Dream Come True

When Pharaoh's wise men and magicians failed to interpret his dreams, the chief butler suddenly remembered Joseph. He recounted to Pharaoh the prison dreams and the accurate interpretation given by a Hebrew prisoner (Genesis 41:9-13). Pharaoh, who was out of options, called for the prisoner.

Joseph's liberation points us to a second vital spiritual principle: Godly character is unaffected by the harsh circumstances of life. Despite years of imprisonment and unfair treatment, Joseph stepped forward with dignity, humility, and faith (Genesis 41:14-16).

Dignity: "He shaved" (Egyptians were clean shaven) and he "changed his clothing" (v. 14). Joseph dressed in appropriate clothes to come before the king. He had a sense of propriety and decorum that years in prison could not erase.

Humility: "It is not in me" (v. 16). Joseph

didn't use the situation for self-promotion. He didn't try to exalt himself as he had earlier in his life (Genesis 37:5–10). Through all that had happened, he had learned to put his trust in the Lord, not in himself.

Faith: "God will give Pharaoh an answer" (v. 16). That sounds like something Daniel (2:27–30) and Paul (Acts 26) would say in the future. Joseph expressed his faith and gave the glory to God.

God's patient investment in the life of Joseph was now paying dividends. And Joseph's patient response revealed that he was learning to overcome life's challenges with dignity, humility, and faith.

> *"No man can at the same time prove that he is clever and that Jesus Christ is mighty to save."*
> —JAMES DENNEY, SCOTTISH THEOLOGIAN (1856-1917)

53

A Dreamer at Work

Pharaoh described his dreams to Joseph, and God, through Joseph, interpreted those dreams (Genesis 41:17–36). As had been the case with Joseph in Canaan and the butler and baker in prison, the dreams came in pairs.

In the first dream, the scene was the Nile River (viewed as a god by ancient Egypt), and seven healthy cows were enjoying the cool water of the river. Suddenly, seven diseased cows, thin and ravaged, came upon the healthy cows and devoured them, without making any difference in the appearance of the diseased cows. This would have been a terrifying thing to witness—cows don't eat beef, they *are* beef!

In the second dream, seven healthy stalks of grain were likewise consumed by seven windblown and dry stalks of grain. This also would have been frightening, for the inanimate stalks of grain were taking on the behavior of living things!

Two dreams—but, as Joseph would reveal, one message.

Joseph challenged Pharaoh to see the purposes of God and to plan accordingly: "God has shown Pharaoh what He is about to do" (v. 25).

The ultimate lesson Joseph had learned through slavery, imprisonment, and mistreatment was that God is in control. He had learned to rest in the sovereignty and faithfulness of God. Now he could say with confidence that if God said it, it would happen. Pharaoh's dreams would be fulfilled because God is God.

Joseph boldly offered counsel to the ruler of the land of Egypt, and it was wise counsel indeed. He told Pharaoh to plan for the lean years by being frugal during the plentiful years.

Pharaoh then made a decision that would dramatically change the ancient world. He appointed Joseph to oversee the food supplies of all Egypt. Why? Because he saw in Joseph

55

not only the qualities of leadership, but, more importantly, that Joseph was "a man in whom is the Spirit of God" (v. 38).

Once again God's timing was perfect. Two years earlier, Joseph's ability to interpret dreams would have been a novelty. Now, his wisdom and discernment were a national treasure.

Joseph was raised to the position God had promised in his dream so many years before (Genesis 37). He was put in charge of the whole land of Egypt. And God had prepared him well for the task ahead of him. He was ready for:

"Not every man can carry a full cup. Sudden elevation frequently leads to pride and a fall. The most exacting test of all is to survive prosperity."
—J. OSWALD SANDERS

- **Perseverance:** It would not be easy for a Hebrew to rule Egypt. The pressure would be intense, especially as the famine wore on.
- **Performance:** The skills Joseph had learned in smaller duties would now be applied to a major task.
- **Pride:** Having fallen once from a high place, Joseph no doubt now understood the fleeting nature of temporal positions and honors.

Joseph was ready for the pressure and the responsibility. He would overcome because God had prepared him, and he was ready to be used of God.

Overcoming Bitterness

A nd so Joseph, at the age of thirty, became the second most powerful man in Egypt—a country that had power and influence far beyond its own borders. He had absolute control over the destinies of millions of people, including the brothers who had sold him into slavery years earlier.

Much had happened since he rose to power. For Joseph, in a sense, all things had become new. In addition to his new position (vice president of the planet earth!), he had been given a new name (Zaphnath Paanea, which means "the one to whom God reveals secrets"). He now had a wife (Azenath) and two sons, whose names revealed the spiritual journey Joseph had been on: Manasseh, which means "forgetting," because God's grace had helped Joseph to forget the pain he had suffered at the hands of his brothers; and Ephraim, which means "fruitful," speaking of the great blessings God had given him in this foreign land.

Forgetful and Fruitful are great names. In fact, Bible teacher J. Vernon McGee referred to them as Amnesia and Ambrosia!

The seven years of plenty predicted by Pharaoh's dreams had come and gone, and Joseph's plan had worked perfectly. The grain was stored, and now, in the midst of the seven years of worldwide famine, the world was coming to Pharaoh's (and to Joseph's) doorstep seeking food—including Joseph's brothers (Genesis 42).

When the famine struck the land of Canaan, word went out that there was food available in Egypt. Soon Jacob sent his ten sons (but not Benjamin, Joseph's only full brother and Jacob's new favorite) to Egypt to try to get enough grain to keep them alive through the famine. There, the brothers stood before Joseph, Pharaoh's chief administrator.

When Joseph was sold into slavery, his brothers had been older, weather-beaten Bedouins, and their appearance had not changed much in the ensuing twenty years. Joseph's appearance, however, had changed dramatically. He had matured from a youth of seventeen to a man in his late thirties, with the appearance of an Egyptian. And, most importantly, he had gone from a slave to a ruler. Joseph immediately recognized his brothers, but not in a million years would they have recognized him!

Joseph questioned them, and tested them. When he discovered that his father and younger brother, Benjamin, were still alive, he set the wheels in motion for a reunion. He sensed that his brothers had changed, but for the sake of

Benjamin, he had to make sure. He forced them to return to Egypt with Benjamin and prepared a final test for them. Joseph knew what God had done in his own heart in Egypt, but he now wanted to find out if God had also been at work in Canaan.

At a lavish banquet, Joseph gave Benjamin five times more than the other brothers, yet they didn't resent the kind of favoritism that they had despised so viciously years earlier when it was directed at Joseph. Then he seemed to put Benjamin in harm's way, testing whether they would protect their youngest brother, or abandon him as they had abandoned Joseph twenty years earlier.

Only God can look at the heart (1 Samuel 16:7), so Joseph devised a final test that would reveal how genuine their apparent change really was.

A Plan for the Test (44:1–13)

After the feast, Joseph commanded his butler to do several things: Fill his brothers' sacks with food, return their money, and put his silver cup in Benjamin's bag.

Joseph would test their character by putting them in the position of having to choose between rescuing Benjamin at great personal risk or abandoning him to slavery for personal gain.

As soon as the brothers departed for Canaan, Joseph sent his servants after them to accuse them of the theft of the cup. The brothers reacted with shock and confusion. They would never do such a thing! Hadn't they returned the money they had found in their bags on the first trip? And they backed up their claims of honesty with a bold offer to prove their innocence and sincerity: "Kill the guilty one, and enslave the rest!" They would certainly not make such an offer if even one of them was guilty.

The steward's reply raised the stakes—and the pressure: "Only the guilty will be enslaved."

Imagine the mounting tension as one by one the sacks were examined, and one by one found to contain only grain. The steward moved from elder to younger, until finally he arrived at Benjamin's donkey.

Imagine the shock and dismay as the cup was found in Benjamin's sack. How could it be? They were so certain of their innocence. "Then they tore their clothes" (v. 13). In this dramatic gesture of mourning, the sons of Jacob displayed the depth of their grief and despair. They responded to Benjamin's distress the same way Jacob had responded years before when he was shown the bloody tunic that had belonged to Joseph.

The agreement was that only the guilty would be enslaved. The easy thing to do would be to leave Benjamin and go home. But they didn't. Envy and resentment no longer governed their thoughts and deeds. They returned to Egypt with Benjamin, determined that whatever was to be faced they would face together.

A Plea for Mercy (44:14–34)

For Joseph, the evidence was clear. His brothers were truly changed men.

- "They fell before [Joseph] on the ground," fulfilling the promise of Joseph's dreams.
- "How shall we clear ourselves? God has found out the iniquity of your servants." They made no excuses or rationalizations, no attempt to cover up. They admitted, through Judah, their guilt and submitted themselves to slavery. It was "we," not "he." Joseph tested them further with an offer of release, and they passed with flying colors.
- "Let [me] remain instead of the lad," begged Judah. What a turnabout! Out of

concern for their father, the same Judah who had been ringleader in the plan to sell Joseph to the slave traders now offered to be Benjamin's substitute as a slave in Egypt. He openly acknowledged that the young man was now Jacob's favorite. But instead of resenting Benjamin's favorite-son status, he longed to preserve it by giving himself.

> *"By their fruits you will know them."*
> —JESUS, MATTHEW 7:20

65

The change in Judah was real. While God had been at work in Joseph's life, He had also been working in Judah and his brothers.

A Passionate Reunion (45:1–15)

For Joseph, the years of pain dissolved in a moment of joy, and he wept uncontrollably in the presence of his brothers. They were tears of joy because his brothers had truly changed, and tears of love because at last they were as brothers should be.

The room was electric as Joseph finally said the words he had longed to say since he first saw his brothers coming before him to ask for food: "I am Joseph."

But they were terrified. The dream had come true. Joseph had the power of life and death over them. What would he do?

Notice his tenderness toward them:

- "He wept aloud," openly expressing his emotion.
- "Please come near to me," he said, wanting them near. They had been apart far too long.
- "Do not . . . be grieved or angry with yourselves." This was not a time for guilt or self-condemnation. This was a time for joy.

- "God sent me," he testified. They were to trust that God was in control.
- "Go . . . and bring my father" he said urgently. It was time to share the joy and reunite the family.

"Then he fell on his brother Benjamin's neck and wept, and Benjamin wept on his neck. Moreover he kissed all his brothers and wept over them, and after that his brothers talked with him."

Forgiveness resolved the issue of guilt. "Joseph displayed his deep faith in the omnipotence of God—overriding Satan, demonic powers, and wicked men to work out His sovereign will and unfrustratable plan. Faith lifted the whole sordid crime out of the pit of misery and self-recrimination and placed it on the mountain peak of divine sovereignty where God's forgiving grace not only heals but wipes away the past and the pain" (Merrill Unger, *Unger's Commentary on the Old Testament*, Moody Press, 1981, p. 94).

Joseph had overcome treachery, temptation, disappointment, the past, and, finally, bitterness—the potential bitterness that would have seemed so normal after all that he had suffered. He exemplified grace, giving full forgiveness and exacting no revenge. He exemplified love, discarding the wrongs of the past for the compassion of the present. He exemplified faith, trusting that God would preserve him from the bitterness that leads to self-destruction.

How could he love the brothers who had so cruelly betrayed him, even to the point of plotting his death? It was through a spirit of mercy born out of grace. It was through love born not out of ease or comfort or convenience, but out of suffering and hardship.

The only way to overcome bitterness is to trust God and rest in Him, because we believe in a

God who is big enough to work in all things for our good.

These are the lessons we learn from the life of Joseph.

The Trust That
Overcomes

I n Genesis 50:20, we read Joseph's final words
to his brothers—words that so beautifully sum
up his life and his faith: "As for you, you meant
evil against me; but God meant it for good, in or-
der to bring it about as it is this day, to save many
people alive." This is the amazing perspective of
a man who embraced the living God and trusted
Him completely.

As you face the pains and heartaches and
mistreatments of life, know that it is only by
complete confidence in the goodness and plan of
God that you can overcome. Then the things that
could destroy you can become building blocks on

the journey of faith as you look for the hand of God in all the circumstances of life.

If you have never confessed your sin and trusted Jesus Christ as your Lord and Savior, life can be a jumbled ball of confusion. But the One who died for your sins and gave Himself for your failures can bring rightness with God, forgiveness of sin, and a new sense of wholeness and purpose into your weary soul. Christ came into the world because of His love for you, and that love can bring an end to the emptiness or bitterness or sinfulness that wracks your life.

> *"This is the victory that has overcome the world—our faith."*
> —1 JOHN 5:4

Accept by faith the gift of eternal life and personal forgiveness He offers, for the only way to really overcome forever is to accept the victory of Calvary that He accomplished for you.

71

"The gift of God is eternal life in Christ Jesus our Lord" (Romans 6:23). Now that is real victory—and real overcoming.

FOR PERSONAL REFLECTION

NOTES

FOR PERSONAL REFLECTION

NOTES

NOTES

FOR PERSONAL REFLECTION

NOTES